Families

Foster Parents

Rebecca Rissman

www.raintreepublishers.co.uk
Visit our website to find out
more information about
Raintree books.

To order:

☎ Phone 0845 6044371

🖹 Fax +44 (0) 1865 312263

🖱 Email myorders@raintreepublishers.co.uk

Customers from outside the UK please telephone +44 1865 312262

Raintree is an imprint of Capstone Global Library Limited, a company incorporated in England and Wales having its registered office at 7 Pilgrim Street, London, EC4V 6LB – Registered company number: 6695582

Text © Capstone Global Library Limited 2011
First published in hardback in 2011
The moral rights of the proprietor have been asserted.

Edited by Rebecca Rissman, Dan Nunn, and Catherine Veitch
Designed by Ryan Frieson
Picture research by Tracy Cummins
Production by Victoria Fitzgerald
Originated by Capstone Global Library
Printed and bound in China by Leo Paper Products Ltd

ISBN 978 1 406 22147 3
14 13 12 11 10
10 9 8 7 6 5 4 3 2 1

British Library Cataloguing in Publication Data
Rissman, Rebecca.
Foster parents. -- (Families)
306.8'74-dc22

Acknowledgements
We would like to thank the following for permission to reproduce photographs: AP Photo pp. 11 (Imaginechina), 17 (John Froschauer); Corbis pp. 4 (©David P. Hall), 6 (©Ann Summa), 8 (©Kevin Dodge), 15, 18 (©Edward Bock); **23c** (©David P. Hall); Getty Images pp. 5 (Tom Stoddar), 7 (Charlie Schuck), **10** (Jon Riley), 12 (Robert Gallagher), 14 (DK Stock/David Deas), 21 (Camille Tokerud), 22 (Jeremy Woodhouse), **23a** (Jon Riley); istockphoto pp. 9 (©Alexander Shalamov), 19 (©Tomasz Markowski), 20 (©Aldo Murillo); Shutterstock pp. 13 (©BlueOrange Studio), 16 (©Golden Pixels LLC), **23b** (©BlueOrange Studio).

Front cover photograph of a family by a lake reproduced with permission of Getty Images (Robert Gallagher). Back cover photograph of a mother and child reproduced with permission of Shutterstock (©BlueOrange Studio).

We would like to thank Anne Pezalla, Dee Reid and Diana Bentley for their invaluable help in the preparation of this book.

Every effort has been made to contact copyright holders of material reproduced in this book. Any omissions will be rectified in subsequent printings if notice is given to the publisher.

Contents

What is a family?

A family is a group of people who care for each other.

People in families are called
family members.

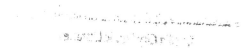

All families are different.

All families are special.

What are families like?

Some families are big.

Some families are small.

What is foster care?

Foster care makes sure children are cared for.

Foster care puts children with
new families.

Who are foster parents?

Foster children's new parents are called foster parents.

Foster parents care for the children.

Some foster parents care for children for a long time.

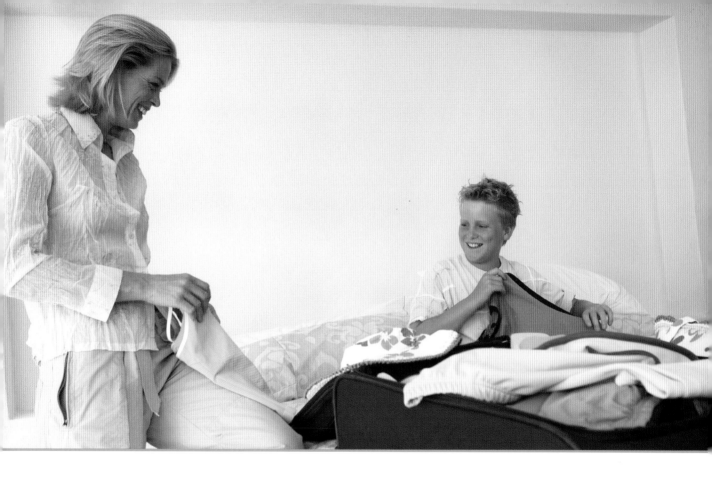

Some foster parents care for children
for a short time.

Some foster parents care for
one child.

Some foster parents care for more
than one child.

Children living with foster parents

Foster parents care for children whose parents could not care for them.

18

Foster parents do all they can to make the children feel happy.

Some children leave their
foster parents to live with their
(20) parents again.

Some children leave their foster parents to live with new families.

Do you know?

Do you know any foster parents?

Picture glossary

 **foster care** puts children with new families

 **foster parent** adult who looks after children that are not their own

 **member** person who belongs to a group

Index

Note to parents and teachers

Before reading

Explain to children that foster care is a special system that makes sure all children are cared for and safe. Some children are in foster care for a short time, and then return to their families. Other children are in foster care until they can be adopted by new families. Explain that adoption is a system that places children with new families.

After reading

Discuss with children how foster parents help children in need. Some children in foster care require special attention that their parents may not have been able to give them. Other children in foster care were not able to live with their parents because they were not safe there.